Dip It! Tap It!

Written by Greg Cook
Photographed by Tim Platt

Collins

Dan tips it in a tin.

Sam tips it in a pan.

Sam dips in a pad.

Sam pats it.

Dan dips in a pad.

Dan taps it.

It is Dad!

Dan dips a pad in a tin.

Dan pats it.

Sam dips it in.

Sam tips it.

It is Nan!

Dad

Nan

Ideas for reading

Written by Clare Dowdall PhD
Lecturer and Primary Literacy Consultant

Learning objectives: read simple words by sounding out and blending the phonemes all through the word from left to right; read a range of familiar and common words and simple sentences independently; hear and say sounds in words in the order in which they occur; show an understanding of how information can be found in non-fiction texts to answer questions about where, who, why and how; extend their vocabulary, exploring the meanings and sounds of new words

Curriculum links: Creative development: Exploring media and materials

Focus phonemes: t, i, p, n, d, a, s, m

Word count: 51

Getting started

- Read the title. Add sound buttons and practise blending the sounds to read *Dip It! Tap It!* together.

- Look at the picture on the front cover together. Ask children to describe what the children are doing.

- Read the blurb together. Help children to say the sounds in the right order, blend the sounds, and reread each sentence fluently.

Reading and responding

- Open the books. Read pp2–3 together. Challenge children to add sound buttons to each child's name.

- Discuss what the children are doing in the pictures and support children's vocabulary for new words, e.g. pour, tray, glitter.

- Ask children to read to p13 aloud. Encourage them to blend phonemes to read new words and reread each sentence fluently.

- Listen as children read. Praise children for blending through words and rereading for fluency.